GPS

How to Get God's Direction

Creative Force Press

Creative Force Press

GPS: How to Get God's Direction
© 2013 by Dave Minton
www.go2ccc.org

This title is also available as an eBook. Visit www.CreativeForcePress.com/titles for more information.

Published by Creative Force Press
4704 Pacific Ave, Suite C, Lacey, WA 98503
www.CreativeForcePress.com

ISBN: 978-1-939989-08-6

Printed in the USA - For worldwide distribution

ENDORSEMENTS

"God's will for every Christian is that they know how to get His direction. Today, there can be so many spiritual detours, distractions, and misguidance. Pastor Dave Minton's new book, GPS: How to Get God's Direction, is not only refreshing and inspiring, but timely.

God has a plan, purpose and pursuit for every believer, and if applied, this book will produce the "good success" that God longs for us to experience. Pastor Dave's wisdom, personal experiences, biblical and practical insight will build your spiritual walk and confidence.

Pastor Dave unlocks a profound biblical truth with a clarity and insight that will stir your desire to grow. This powerful message is not just an option, but an opportunity for every Christian to take their walk with Christ to the next level."

–Pastor Art Sepulveda, Author & Senior Pastor Word of Life Christian Center, Hawaii

"Dave Minton has led his own family and church by learning to be led by the Holy Spirit. His ministry has grown through some of life's greatest challenges. He is one of those men we can follow by example."

–Casey Treat, Author & Senior Pastor of Christian Faith Center, Federal Way, WA

"Dave's book is like opening up my TomTom GPS for the first time. That amazing TomTom has kept me on the right path so many times. But I did have to learn how to use it. My parents for years had a GPS in their car, yet they still were getting lost with the fold-out maps. Just because you have a GPS, doesn't mean you will get to the right spot. You have to use it.

This incredible book shows you how to use the Holy Spirit like the GPS of life. The Holy Spirit guides and directs you right where God wants you to go. But just like the TomTom, you need to know how to use it. Dave's book gives you the step by step guide to being led by the Spirit. If you are sick of getting lost in life, I highly encourage you to read this book."

–**Pastor Scot Anderson**, Author of *Think Like a Billionaire, Become a Billionaire: As a Man Thinks, So is He*

"My long-time friend, Dave Minton, is a man unwavering in his faith and one who has devoted his life to seeking God's direction in both the good and the more difficult times in his own life. In GPS, Dave will help readers navigate through life with an understanding of God's plans for them. They will learn how they can make the right decisions and access His direction for their everyday life."

–**Pastor Leon Fontaine**, Senior Pastor Springs Church, Canada, and CEO of Miracle Channel

DEDICATION

I DEDICATE THIS BOOK TO
MY LEADER, THE GREATEST
LEADER OF ALL,
CHRIST.

TABLE OF CONTENTS

Small Group & Bible Study Questions

A PERSONAL MESSAGE FROM PASTOR DAVE MINTON

As a pastor, I'm often asked questions like,

"How do I know God's will?"
"How do I know if this is the right decision or not?"
"How can I figure out what He has for me?"
"What is His plan for my life?"

Have you ever asked these questions? My heart's desire for you as you read *GPS: How to Get God's Direction* is for you to have a clear idea of how God leads and guides you. As His children, God has an expectation of us; an expectation that we understand and know His will.

"For as many as are led by the Spirit of God are the sons of God" (Romans 8:14). Here's what I want you to understand: you need to have a *real* confidence and know that God wants to lead you. You have to believe that God wants you to know His will, and that He will direct your path.

Do you remember how you used to get directions before you had a smartphone or a GPS? Before you got one of these handy devices, you'd get out a paper map, unfold it, spread it out, and try to figure out

"*Where am I on this?*" first, and then locate your desired destination.

It was a common sight: seeing people pulled over on the side of the road with their maps spread out. If it were me, and I knew where I wanted to go, but couldn't decipher the map, what would my wife always want me to do? Stop and ask for directions.

When you stop and ask the gas station attendant or the convenience store clerk, you say, "Can you give me directions to get to this place...?"

They look at you strangely, "Yeah, it's down the road maybe 3, 4, maybe 6 stop lights."

Not super helpful.

They continue with, "It's kinda down...in...that direction," and they point.

So, you get back in the car and your wife says, "Did they give you directions?"

"Umm, yes, and now we need to ask somebody else."

You drive 3 or 4 streets more, and someone else starts giving you landmarks. "There's a red house on the left, and when you go past that, you'll see the neighbor who has llamas in the yard, but they're not really llamas." Asking for directions and guidance to safely arrive at your destination in a timely manner can be difficult! You know what I'm talking about!

On the road, we're looking for external guidance. But, thank God—I'm grateful for the invention of GPS. On the road of life, God wants to lead you and have you understand His will through an internal GPS: His Spirit.

I pray that through reading this book you will have clear understanding of, and be equipped to, be led by the Holy Spirit in your daily life.

C'mon somebody!

Pastor Dave Minton

Introduction

Seven Ways God Leads Us

"When He, the Spirit of truth, has come, He will guide you into all truth; for He will not speak on His own authority, but whatever He hears He will speak; and He will tell you things to come." –John 16:13

When you have an internal guidance system that you've learned to trust and rely on, you know you will arrive at the correct destination; God's destination. The key is to know how to discern that guidance system's voice.

This book, *GPS*, is full of examples and biblical wisdom on learning to be led by God's Spirit. As we get started, I'd like to define the seven ways in which He leads us.

In a multitude of counsel, there is safety, and even the Holy Spirit uses a variety of "counsels." When we learn to recognize the various ways in which He leads us and speaks, we can grow in our confidence in recognizing His voice.

The Holy Spirit works in, and through, all of these methods:

1. He leads us by His Spirit.
2. He leads us by His Word.
3. He leads us by our human spirit.
4. He leads us by counsel and correction.
5. He leads us by the gifts of the Spirit.
6. He leads us by spectacular manifestations.
7. He leads us by challenges and opportunities.

Let's break each one down a bit further.

1. He leads us by His Spirit.

Learn how to recognize His promptings and the inner voice and the inner dialog of the Holy Spirit. The inner dialog is the most common way you're going to be led; it's internally by God's Spirit, His promptings, His guidance. He will teach you, and He's going to bring the Word to your remembrance.

I'd like to tell you about a time when I was driving, and I had an encounter with God in my car. Later in this book I will tell this story in more detail, but I will summarize it now and use it as a direct example of how God's Spirit leads us. I had been frustrated about trying to build His church, and He said to me, "I didn't ask you to build My church." I replied, "Then what do you want me to do?" He said, "I want you to make disciples." I said, "Okay, well, fine, that'll be easy, so that's what I'll do."

Within days, a gentleman came up to me, "Are you the Pastor?" and we ended up buying some nearby apartments from him. I wasn't interested in apartments, nor was I seeking to purchase apartments. Almost before I could say no, I felt a prompting on the inside that said, "Go with this idea." We ended up buying those apartments with no money down, and I still wasn't sure why. Shortly after, we were contacted by an agency that said, "We have a program for young adults coming out of prison and homelessness, and we want to bring these at-risk kids into your apartment complex." They even helped us get a grant to remodel it. Their unique program included a counselor living in one of the apartments, so the kids could have independence and have somebody there to provide coaching, support and accountability. Later we sold the apartment building to that agency.

After I shared that story at a Sunday service, a young woman came up to me and introduced herself. She said, "I'm glad you told that story. After you sold that building, I started coming to this church…that was *my* program. I was one of those kids." And I said, "Tell me the rest of the story." So she began to tell me things like how many kids have been impacted by that program, how it's become so successful that other organizations use it as a model, and that they've received well over a million dollars in grants to duplicate the program throughout our county. All this came about by listening to a simple prompting of the Holy Spirit.

I was thrilled to hear how this story played out. I

wonder, though, how many times we won't get to hear the rest of the story; when we've been obedient to His voice and what happens as a result. Perhaps we won't get to hear many things until heaven, but trust me...there will be stories attached to your obedience. What about that person you invited to church? Maybe they didn't actually show up, but may end up in church sometime in the future. How about that person you prayed for and maybe never saw them again? There is a *rest of the story*. If you will learn to recognize the promptings of the Spirit of God, it will impact your life in some incredible ways.

2. He leads us by His Word.

Promptings that we sense *always* need to come into alignment with God's Word. This is how we can understand, have safety and have security in these promptings of God. It's important to renew our minds with God's Word and not to trust our emotions. Instead, depend upon the Word of God for counsel and guidance.

The Bible says in Psalm 119, "Thy Word is a lamp unto my feet and a light unto my path." God will reveal to you how you should proceed as you're being led by His Word. In fact, often throughout scripture, there were supernatural manifestations that would bring them back to the Word of God. When God appeared and began to speak to Joshua (in Joshua 1), telling him he is now His servant, what does He tell Joshua to do? God tells Joshua to meditate on His Word. "This book of the law shall not depart from your mouth, but you should meditate in it day and night, for then you will make your way prosperous and then you will have a good success" (Joshua 1:8).

Now catch this: Joshua is talking to God and God is saying, "Read My Word." How often do people want to do things and make decisions contrary to God's Word? They'll justify it and say, "Well, I prayed about it. Doesn't He want me to be happy?"

It usually comes down to that: happiness. Does He want us to be happy? No, He wants us to be obedient. Have you ever seen a parent try to raise a *happy* child? Let's just keep little Johnny happy...but he ends up self-centered, obnoxious, mean, and cruel. An obedient child is a blessed child. The more you try to make a child happy, the more unhappy behavior will come out as they try to get their selfish needs met. So, no, His goal for you and I is not to be *happy*. He wants our obedience.

Instead, when we are obedient, here's what we get: joy. Joy is a deep passion, joy is a strength, joy is an ability, joy is based on (no matter what's going on in life) the joy of the Lord. Jesus said, "I'll give you My joy." Jesus, Himself, went through many trials, but for the joy set before Him, even endured the cross. So we need the guidance of the Word.

3. He leads us by our human spirit.

You have a spirit, and God can't write His law on your heart unless you're born again, but once you are born again, new desires start growing in your heart. Even so, the Bible says that we still have to intentionally grow our spirits.

Like our physical bodies need exercise, our spirits need strength training, too. We have to learn how to desire the sincere milk of the Word, to renew our minds, grow in our capacity to love, and to live generously, as a few examples. When it comes to hearing Him clearly, some of us will never learn God's will because we don't engage in serving God's purposes and exercising our spirits.

The Bible says, in fact, that if we don't exercise or practice doing the will of God or following the Word of God, we will digress and need milk again. We'll have to be put in spiritual convalescent care or go back to the nursery to be fed because we can't feed ourselves!

In the book of Hebrews it says that the Spirit will speak to us through the desires of our hearts. What is in your heart? Whatever is in it will come out, good or bad. Matthew 12:33-35 talks about the good desires of our heart brings forth good things. The evil man, out of the desire of his heart, brings forth evil things. The Spirit will speak to us about those good things within, through our conscience. If we learn to recognize how our own spirit speaks to us, we'll know if something is a desire of the flesh, or a desire of the Spirit.

The Bible says there is none good; no one, only God.

So, you might ask, "How can I bring forth good things out of my heart unless I become a new creation, old things have passed away, and all things have become new?" By learning how to recognize the good things in your heart. You have a calling from God, but most people are afraid to say yes to God, because they're afraid God will ask them to do something they don't want to do. In reality, the calling of God is to make you to become who you were created to be.

When God called Gideon, He was calling Gideon to be his true self. When God called Moses, He was calling Moses to be his true self. When He called Abraham, He was calling Abraham to be his true self. And, the same goes for Mary, Peter, Paul, and countless others. Most of us are afraid to become who we really are, but this fear would wane once you knew how to develop your spirit. Since your spirit is subject to your soul, to be sure your spirit isn't just tagging along with wherever your soul wants to go, renew that soul, that mind, with the Word. If your soul isn't renewed, your spirit will always be pulled along, versus being led by your spirit that's being led by God's Spirit.

4. He leads us by counsel and correction.

In a multitude of counselors, there is safety. Do you have people, trusted people, who you receive counsel and correction from? Here's a thought: if you're not receiving any correction in your life, you might not be in the will of God. Moses speaks to the burning bush and is corrected on his way to Egypt. Moses' father-in-law tells him that what he is doing is not good. He doesn't listen to his father-in-law, and a few chapters later in Numbers, God himself tells him the same thing.

Peter has God-breathed revelation and says, "You are the Christ," then a few moments later, Jesus turns around and says to Peter, "You're full of the devil." Jonah is running from God and that makes his life miserable. Esther is in the kingdom, and her uncle Mordecai comes and says, "Look, sis, you might have a silver spoon in your mouth right now and fancy surroundings, parading around like you're somebody, but I'm telling you you're here for such a time as this." Everybody needs an Uncle Mordecai in our life when we start to live too easy.

The Bible refers to wisdom as the Spirit of God. Wisdom *is* the Spirit. The Bible also says if you do not receive correction, wisdom will stop speaking to you. But here's the cool part: If I am a son, I get corrected. Some of us are afraid to move forward for fear of messing up, right? If you're afraid of going forward because you're afraid of messing up, you've already messed up! It's better to go forward and mess up, then allow God to correct you. That's a better way. I pray, "I'm going forward God, Your Word says *go*! I'm going!"

5. He leads us by the gifts of the Spirit.

The Bible says we should pursue love and desire

spiritual gifts, and not to be ignorant of them. Some of us are ignorant of the gifts, things like prophesy, word of knowledge, and word of wisdom. If we haven't been taught, we don't really understand them yet. But here's what you need to understand about them first; they should never be for direction. They should always be for confirmation. And, we should never put that person who gives those gifts to us *ahead* of the message itself.

In other words, never elevate the person who's saying it to you above the One who is above all things. Who is the Master?

If I get a word of wisdom for you, my job is to hear from God and speak to you. But, every time God speaks to me and through me, it can get tainted, and get a little of my flavor or personality with it. The Bible says that a prophecy is subject to the prophet. Think of it like a garden hose that's been lying in the sun. Water comes into it from the source, but by the time it comes out the other end, it will still quench your thirst, but it's got a rubbery flavor to it.

6. He leads us by spectacular manifestations.

I never *seek* manifestations, but God can and does lead us by them. They're often used to prepare us for real, pending adversity that's ahead of us. In fact, sometimes the more spectacular the manifestation, the more it is a preparation for what's on our road ahead. For example, when God spoke to Paul out of heaven, it was to tell him what great things he must suffer for

Christ's sake.

I've had a few encounters with God that I would refer to as *spectacular manifestations*, and they were to confirm to me and witness to me that God was with me for what was in my future.

7. He leads us by challenges and opportunities.

It would be easy to look at Joseph's life and believe he was totally out of the will of God. Slavery, accusation, jail, yet all the while, God was in every step of leading him through all the trials. Later in life, Joseph understood that what his brothers meant for evil, God meant it for good.

Some of you might be going through difficult circumstances, but it's all about God getting you into the right position. He's positioning you for something according to His purposes. So, be careful in trials—if you don't have the right attitude, you can get to the point where bitterness takes over. For Joseph to release what God wanted him to do, he could not stay bitter. Don't let the processes of life make you bitter. Stay on your feet—it's not over!

As you read on, each short chapter will teach and demonstrate how you can begin your journey of being led by God's Spirit.

STAY OUT OF THE DITCH

"Where there is no counsel, the people fall; but in the multitude of counselors there is safety."
–Proverbs 11:14

Let's be honest; most people think hearing God's voice is hard. Most people are not sure what it even means, and many are confused about it. That's not God's will for your life. He wants you to know and clearly understand His will. *That* is His agenda for your life.

First, I'd like to mention something that can get in the way, become a stumbling block or hindrance to discerning or hearing His voice. One problem is that people can get into extremes when following God. Out in the country, for every mile of road, there's two miles of ditches. We want to stay out of both of them.

In one ditch, there are people who are just relying on emotion. They just *feel* God leading and guiding them, and yes, we do at times feel and sense God leading and guiding us. But for some, it really becomes more of an emotional leading, not a spiritual leading. This causes people to make rash decisions or make decisions that won't really work out for them.

One time, I had a person tell me her daughter was pregnant. She said, "God told me that my daughter's child is going to be a girl." So she went out and spent a lot of money buying lots of girl stuff. Later, she came back and said, "Pastor, why did God tell me that it was going to be a girl, and then it wasn't a girl?" I said, "That's easy – it wasn't God." This same person later on went to an auction and bought a whole bunch of used cars and planned to re-sell them. The result was her losing a lot of money. She continued to do a series of things like that, and became offended at God and offended at church. It derailed her life. She was making *emotional decisions* in the name of God.

We've all seen that ditch.

In the other ditch, you get the very analytical, cerebral people. For them, it must all line up, and all the facts have to be there; emotion is not involved. If it's not crystal clear, they're not moving; not until everything is all in order. Often, this person doesn't really do *anything* by faith at all. They don't know what it is to experience and be comfortable with promptings and leadings of the Spirit of God in their lives.

Both ditches operate out of a spiritual ignorance: not knowing or clearly understanding how God wants to lead and guide us. God wants to guide us in every area of our lives by His Spirit. Think about that. God wants to lead and guide you in every area of your life by His Spirit!

EMOTION AND INTELLIGENCE

"For the word of God is living and powerful, and sharper than any two-edged sword, piercing even the division of soul and spirit, and of joints and marrow, and is a discerner of the thoughts and intents of the heart." –Hebrews 4:12

Because it's one of the biggest challenges people of faith have when attempting to hear God's Spirit, I want to share more examples of the emotional and intellectual ditches. But, again, when we talk about being led by the Spirit, it is very emotional in the way God leads us. Because of this, we have to be able to discern whether this is our own emotion or God's Spirit leading and guiding.

Often what happens is people don't process their own emotions well, nor do many of us handle conflict well. So, in learning how to work out and process emotions, they just label it as God leading them to get away from their problems. That makes for a very unstable life because they're constantly chasing the greener grass or the least amount of conflict. When God's leading us, it's to take us right through adversity and conflict with the confidence that He's with us. It is important to recognize some kind of emotion or conflict exists in this process.

If I got up each Sunday and asked myself if I felt led to come to church, most likely I wouldn't directly *feel* a special leading. If I'm convinced that God was leading me by what my own spirit or emotions feel, in all honesty, I could easily determine that He wasn't leading me to go. Obviously, that's not a true way to be led by God. There are other ways He guides me, and some include the faith-based commitments I've made in my life (like my marriage and pastoring).

We know the other ditch people may fall into is the ditch of intellect. It's not emotional reasoning; it's intellectual reasoning. This person has to have all the facts, all the information, they have to gather all the data, they have to cross the T's and dot the I's. But the problem with this is by the time they have it all figured out, the moment of opportunity may have passed—come and gone.

It is possible to miss the will of God. In other words, sometimes God is giving you a green light to go, and you're still sitting there waiting for results. If you tell me God is leading you, show me some results after you go. If there are no results there, then it's time to really think and pray again about what God is leading you to do. It doesn't mean the results aren't on the way, sometimes, but ultimately sooner or later, there have to be results. That's one of the ways I've validated hearing His voice correctly in my own life.

THE WORKMANSHIP OF GOD

"Before I formed you in the womb I knew you; Before you were born I sanctified you" –Jeremiah 1:5

You know, I love my GPS. I travel a lot. And speaking of traveling, I heard that scientists launched a space probe to Mars and it had to travel 350,000 miles away to reach its destination. It was launched into space, and they landed that thing right where they wanted it to be.

How many know that God throughout the ages has been programming you to land somewhere? Yes, you're the workmanship of God, created in Christ Jesus for good works. God told Jeremiah, "Before you were formed in your mother's womb, I knew you, and I appointed you a prophet to the nations." David said, "Where could I go to get away from your presence? If I were to make my bed in hell you would be there. I could run to the farthest planet, and you would be there, for I am your workmanship. That my soul knows very well." He goes on to talk about how the days are fashioned for us and are written in His book, before they were even materialized.

God has a program in you. You were created with a program in you. And if you and I would tap in to His GPS, if we tap in to His guidance, He will lead and guide us by His Spirit in every area of our lives; in every major decision.

When God leads us by His Spirit, we can really learn how to let go of the tendency to depend on our own emotions and intellect.

YOU ARE NOT LOST

"The steps of a good man are ordered by the Lord, and He delights in his way." –Psalm 37:23

I was in another city a few years ago, and I had a couple of our ministry interns with me, and my son. We arrived a day early, had dinner, and decided to see a movie. I said, "Okay guys, where are we going?" They start looking up directions on their phones. It was confusing.

There we were, in the middle of three or four merging streets, one going this way and the other going that way. We were supposed to turn on First Street but there was more than one First Street. Because of the dot on the GPS, we knew that the first First Street we turned on wasn't the correct First Street we needed to be on. Have you ever been to a city like this? Who designs these roads?

We needed to turn on the *second* First Street. So, we ended up in an industrial area, where there are no people, no cars, and I say, "Okay guys, are you sure we're on the right road? We've obviously been on an alternate route." A GPS will give you more than one route. We could have been lost in this unsafe, industrial area, but then we took a left and *boom*, there's the theater right out of nowhere! Because we had a GPS, and I saw the dot on the course, I knew we were not lost. I had the security of an internal guidance system, and we didn't have to stop and ask anybody.

The next morning, we were on our way to the church. We had never been there before, so we had the address programmed into the phone. But, until you get the dot on the GPS moving, you don't know if you're going in the right direction. You have to start moving to see if you made the right turn or not.

We started off and I say, "Go left," and they go left out of the parking lot. Oops…that was the wrong way. Should we turn around? Nope—it has already found another, alternate route to get us to our destination. There was no need to start over. **Even when I make a bad turn, I'm still not lost.**

Thank God for His internal GPS. The Bible says in Hebrews 8:10, "For this is the covenant that I will make with the house of Israel…" In other words, with us in the new covenant (after Jesus' death), He says, *I will put my GPS on their minds. I will take my GPS and write it upon their hearts. I will be their God, and they shall be My people.* God wants to write His guidance system on the inside of us.

God has written His law on the inside of us. But, the

problem is that we're still old-school. We have the GPS, but we haven't figured out how to use it, so we keep pulling over to the side of the road and pulling out the map, or asking for directions, looking for landmarks, etc., because we didn't take the time to get the right app and put it into the phone.

By the way, you can't use my GPS. Why? Because you don't have my password. If I gave it to you, it wouldn't help you, because you don't have access to it. What I'm trying to encourage you to do is access the GPS that God is trying to equip *you* with and empower *you* with to live in His will. Because when you live in His will, it's a place of peace, joy, and satisfaction; peace and joy in the Holy Ghost!

MULTITUDE OF COUNSELORS

"In a multitude of counselors there is safety."
–Proverbs 11:14

I really believe in the ministry of the Word of God. There are people who are about to make important decisions in their lives. How many know that we can all be led by God's Spirit? And the Bible says where there is no counsel, we'll fall into a ditch, but in a multitude of counselors there is safety.

While we are talking about ways God ministers to us, we should remember to never make major decisions in our lives based on only *one* witness; on only one opinion. Just to be clear, a multitude of counselors is not a whole bunch of people saying the same thing. For example, if all of your family members are against something, that is one counsel. If all the people you work with say the same thing, that's one counsel. God is telling us that in a multitude of counselors or different perspectives there is safety.

In Deuteronomy, it's the law to operate this way.

Thank God we're living under a new covenant since Jesus came, but back in Old Testament times when a major decision was about to be made in taking someone's life, the Word says, "...whoever is deserving of death will be put to death on the testimony of two or three witnesses. He shall not be put to death on the testimony of just one witness." In other words you should not be making major decisions with your life—life-threatening or life-altering decisions—based on one witness. So, it's important that we plug in to wise counsel.

Before you tune your ear to what someone has to say, consider the amount of wisdom that person has in the area you need advice in.

AN EAR TO HEAR

"He who has an ear, let him hear what the Spirit says to the churches." –Revelation 2:7

American Christians are highly individualistic. Knowing that, be careful. Often, because of our individualistic focus, we want to run off and do what God is telling us to do before really listening for God to tell us what He wants the church to do. Wise believers take time to listen with spiritual ears to what the Spirit is saying to His church. If we're not plugged in to what the Spirit is saying to the church, His body as a whole, we start moving out from under the cover of the leadership of the Spirit of God. **Yes, God will lead you individually, but you have to also understand that He is leading the church, first.**

When most people seek the leadership of God, they want to know where to go and what to do. But the leadership of God first says, "Grow." We are excited by salvation and His call, and we want His will to be revealed right away. He says, "Before you go, I want you to grow." From observation, I've never seen people make decisions for their lives as it relates to the will of God without staying in the house (church) where they are growing. Now, I've seen highly spiritually-minded people who are not planted in God's house proceed to make foolish decisions.

In the Word, in Revelation Chapters 2 and 3, John is having an encounter with Jesus. In this encounter, Jesus starts talking about the churches; seven different churches in Asia and the Middle East. The seven churches had different corrections, admonitions, instructions, or certain kinds of things that God wanted them to adjust or address specifically in their church. Jesus also details certain kinds of rewards that would come with their adjustments. To everyone in each church He made this statement, "He who has an ear to hear, let him hear what the Spirit says to the churches." And while you and I are part of the corporate body of Christ, we have our own unique individual assignments. When you and I understand what God wants to do in His church, and we are plugged in to that, we are right in the center of the revelation highway.

"You crown the year with goodness and Your paths drip with abundance" (Psalm 65:11). I feel God all over that verse when I say it. One of the witnesses of the Spirit is His Word. In fact, He *never* leads you contrary to His Word. Don't seek God's blessing; seek the path that He has for the church and you, and you'll find that *this path* is already blessed.

TIMES AND SEASONS

"...the sons of Issachar who had understanding of the times, to know what Israel ought to do, their chiefs were two hundred..." –1 Chronicles 12:32

There are two kinds of people who come to church:
1. Those who need to hear a message from God about what's really going on in their life at the moment, and
2. Another group of people who come who try to hear what God is saying to the church in this season. The first group comes with a legitimate need. The second group comes wanting to learn how to build, integrate and work their life around what God is saying to His church.

As a pastor, I continuously hear stories of God's favor all over people in the congregation. Something unique is happening in people's lives by the Spirit of God. That is what this message is all about. I felt like God was saying to me, "Teach people to listen to My Spirit because there are victories I want to bring forth all over this house. There are stories I want to bring out all over this house. There are things I want to accomplish."

Let's look at a couple of scriptures about times and seasons. 1 Chronicles 12:32 is speaking about sons of Issachar who had special understanding to know what Israel ought to do at that time. There are times when *we* ought to know what to do. Remember when Esther became queen and was getting *promoted*? Her uncle, Mordecai, reminded her that she came into the kingdom for such a time as this. Have you ever considered that the favor on your life is because God is trying to position you for what He wants you to do in the Kingdom?

The Bible says in Ecclesiastes 3 that there is a time for every season and for every purpose under heaven. If you read that chapter, it talks about a time to be born and a time to die, a time to love, a time to hate, a time to sow and a time to reap, a time to plant and a time to pluck up, and it goes on. Then verse 11 says that God has made everything beautiful in its time and has put eternity in our hearts, but no one finds out the works from the beginning to the end. In other words, there's something inside of us, if we were to pursue God and be led by God. **He's going to make things beautiful in our life, in its time.** There are times of sacrificing, but there are also times of plenty. There are times of sowing and there are times of harvest.

There are different times and seasons for us as God's people. It's not about the calendar or the weather. It's about what God wants to do in our lives, in our community, in our country, and in the world.

BE USEABLE

"Also I heard the voice of the Lord, saying: 'Whom shall I send, and who will go for Us?' Then I said, 'Here am I! Send me.'" –Isaiah 6:8

God wants to do something in our hearts, in our communities, in our country, and in the world. Our world is very biblically illiterate even though we are more intellectual and have more information and knowledge than we've ever had in the past. Despite our abundance of information, our families are struggling, we're falling apart, sin is tempting and consuming us, people are messed up, and we're confused. Obviously, worldly knowledge is not the answer.

I sense God saying, "Be a church that I can use. **Be a people that I can use right now.** My path will drip with everything you need: favor, provision, significance."

REDEEM THE TIME

"See that you walk circumspectly, carefully; not as fools but as wise." –Ephesians 5:15

How can we live wisely, not foolishly? By redeeming the time. Think about this: when do most people get serious about changing? When they're in pain. Do you think God would say to someone, "Hey…you might want to change that now…You might not want to go down that path…You might want to avoid that?" Do you think that God might want the opportunity to coach us *before* we felt like changing? Yes, He does.

Redeem the time. What does that mean? It means God wants the best use of my time, as it relates to what the Spirit is saying. What is the witness of the Spirit on my life? How is He leading me right now? My heart's cry to God is, "Help me to redeem my time for the purpose I was created for!"

For example, our worship team produced a worship CD because people were always asking us for one. A few years back, we were in a leader's conference, and someone said, "When are you going to make your

CD?" And I thought, "Now. This year." I looked over at our Worship Pastor, and she said, "Okay." Do you know how stressful that kind of project is for people who've never written and produced songs? Do you realize without redeeming the time, we'd say *one of these days* we're going to…We're planning on doing this project *one of these days*. Without putting it into a real timeframe, there's never a demand on the gift. And some of us, if we don't put a demand on the gift, 'it' never happens.

When are you going to? When are you going to start reading scripture? When are you going to build your prayer life? When are you going to start serving? When are you going to really serve the Lord with passion?

Whatever you do, whenever you serve God's house, give it your best. If it's not your best, you're not redeeming the time; you're wasting it. I've never seen God bless half-hearted efforts, nor have I seen God favor mediocre output. I've never seen God bless someone *helping Him out*, but I have seen God bless whole-heartedness. **Whole-heartedness releases favor.** Ephesians 5 goes on to say, "…the days are evil, therefore do not be unwise but understand what the will of the Lord is." So, for everyone who reads scripture, God expects us to not be foolish, to not waste our time, and to know what His will is. If I don't know His will now, yet He tells me to know it, then it's His responsibility to make it clear to me. That's good news!

GOD'S EXPECTATIONS

"For God has not given us a spirit of fear, but of power and of love and of a sound mind."
–2 Timothy 1:7

What if I told you that God *expects* you to know His will? Ephesians 5:15 says, "See that you walk circumspectly," meaning with intentionality. If you're not living your life with an intentionality to it, you're just showing up, punching time in and punching time out, like going to a job and going through the motions. The Bible calls that living foolishly.

It advises us to, "Be wise and redeem the time." If you're not being intentional, you're wasting time. It goes on to say, "the days are evil. Therefore do not be unwise but understand what the will of the Lord is." If God expects you and I to understand His will, many of us still think, "Wow, but I *don't* know what it is…," and get all jammed up inside. But knowing that expectation, you should encourage yourself, because here's the thought you should take to heart: if God expects me to know His will, then He will help me to know it. That encourages me!

In other words, a lot of people are going to stand before God and hear Him say:

"Why didn't you do something with what I gave you?" "Because I didn't know Your will."
"Why not?"

And do you know what the reason will come down to? Fear. If you were being emotionally led, rather than being led by His Spirit, His will wasn't clearly, accurately discerned. Then, because you were afraid to do the *wrong* thing, you did *nothing*.

When I get to heaven I'd rather hear God say, "Why did you do that?" And I'd say, "Because I thought that was what You wanted." I'd rather move forward and need course corrections along the way than to allow fear to keep me stuck.

THE SPIRIT NUDGES

"With the same measure you use, it will be measured to you, and to you who hear, more will be given."
–Mark 4:24

God makes it clear to us what His will is. Once you start following the Spirit, you will grow in the Spirit's leading and prompting. The Bible says in Mark 4, "If anyone has ears to hear, let him hear," which was the same thing Jesus said to the church in Revelation, and He added, "Take heed what you hear." In other words, He's teaching *how* to listen to the Spirit. "With the same measure you use, it will be measured to you, and to you who hear, more will be given."

Do you understand that once you start learning to recognize how God brings His witness to your spirit, once you understand how God leads you, then the Bible says you'll grow in that. That's exciting. You'll grow in that!

In 1 John 2:20, Jesus says, "But you have an anointing from the Holy One and you know all things." It doesn't mean *you* know all things automatically. It's as if God is talking about the

45

Internet in the first century. God saying, "Just Google me. I will answer your questions for you. I have access to what you need to know."

Now watch this: later in the chapter, John writes, "These things I have written to you concerning those who try to deceive you. But the anointing you have received from Him abides in you and you don't need anyone to teach you." That is golden, but be careful; it's not saying we don't need any teachers, pastors, leaders, mentors, or coaches in life. That would be contrary to the counsel of other parts of God's Word. It really means when you're in a situation where someone is trying to deceive you or take advantage of you, when you're in a situation where someone is not everything they present themselves to be, you don't need anybody to expose them. God's Spirit will tell you. "Something feels wrong. Hmmm…this is a no-go here." Listen to that voice.

Help us Jesus. We, especially young people, need people to help us to recognize the unction of the Spirit; the inner convictions of the Spirit. Once we clearly discern His voice, it's easily recognizable. I can describe it like an internal "check." You feel something holding you back, compelling you not to go further. If you do, you go further at your own peril like choosing to run a red light. **We really need to plug into this before we make decisions.**

On the other end, they can be nudges like a green light and the Holy Spirit says come on, go. Go! The first year of the church, we had a worker who was stealing money from the church. She wrote checks to herself, but our accounts were set up to require two signatures on checks. However, the bank was letting her make one-signature withdrawals. It was a good system, but the bank didn't honor the system. I was in the bank on some personal business one day, and I'm walking out the door, but right before I reached the door, the Spirit of God prompted me to go back and ask them to bring up the checking history.

I walked over and said, "I've got a crazy question. Bring up the account history of the church." And right there were all the single-signature withdrawals, and God exposed that revelation. How did I know that? I didn't. It was the prompting of the Spirit.

I could go on, telling you story after story of how God nudges and God checks. We don't have to be weird about it. I don't run around saying, *"God told me..."* I just get nervous when people tell me that and the fruit or result is not good. I'm not sure if they're trying to convince me or themselves.

In Acts 16, Paul is doing mission work, building churches. When they traveled through Pyrenes and the regions of Galatia, they were forbidden by the Holy Spirit to preach the Word in Asia. After they came to Mica, they tried to go, but the Spirit did not permit them. So, passing by Mica they came to Tora, and, in a night vision, a Macedonian man appeared to Paul and pleaded with him saying, "Come over to Macedonia and help us." Paul responded by immediately heading to Macedonia. He said, "There's a witness of the inner promptings and another dream and vision that occurred. We concluded that the Spirit was telling us to go preach the gospel to them." Are you catching how this works?

On another occasion, in Acts chapter 27, Paul said, "I perceive that if we go out on this journey, not only are we going to lose the cargo and the ship, we're in danger of losing our own lives." Now, Paul was not a coward. He was always facing death. Sure enough, but notice he didn't say to the men, "Hey, the Lord told me there was going to be a storm," but instead, "I *perceive* that..."

Here's what we can learn from this: hearing the prompting of the Spirit doesn't have to be in church. It gives me goose bumps to literally be led by the prompting, and to perceive and conclude the will of God anywhere and at any time.

CUT THROUGH THE CLUTTER

"Then He said, 'Go out, and stand on the mountain before the Lord.'" –1 Kings 19:11

Another example of how God's Spirit speaks is a story about when Elijah was discouraged. 1 Kings 19:9 talks about Elijah going into a cave. When we get discouraged or have setbacks we tend to go into caves, emotionally. "There he went into a cave, and spent the night in that place; and behold, the Word of the Lord came to him, and He said to him, 'What are you doing here, Elijah?' So he said, 'I have been very zealous for the Lord God of hosts; for the children of Israel have forsaken Your covenant, torn down Your altars, and killed Your prophets with the sword. I alone am left; and they seek to take my life.'"

God answered. "Then He said, 'Go out, and stand on the mountain before the Lord.' And behold, the Lord passed by, and a great and strong wind tore into the mountains and broke the rocks in pieces before the Lord, but the Lord was not in the wind; and after the wind an earthquake, but the Lord was not in the earthquake; and after the earthquake a fire, but the Lord was not in the fire; and after the fire a *still small voice*."

If we don't deal with the clutter and distractions in our lives, we'll miss the delicate, gentle prompting and leadings of God. "Suddenly a voice came to him and said, 'What are you doing here, Elijah?'"

I love those verses, so full of symbolism. First, there was a wind, and it was a fierce wind that would push strongly on you. I see a lot of people move in the wrong direction; they feel pushed into it, and they think it's God doing it. Really, they are getting caught up in some kind of gravitational pull; a fad or a movement, because everybody is moving in that direction. I've been a Christian a long time, and I've seen fads come and I've seen fads go; all in the name of the Lord. But the whole time, the Church stands.

Many organizations, groups and traveling events have come and gone, but after they fulfill their mission, their supporters come back to the house. Do not forsake the fellowship and teaching of churches because of fads. Cut the clutter out of your life; the things that would distract you from God's true voice.

God was not in the earthquake, nor was He in the fire. Next to a fire you can get warm and comfortable. Some people's only goal in life is to be comfortable. God is not into being comfortable. Or, fires can get out of the fire pit and devour everything around it, becoming all consuming. People get all consumed with their careers, their dreams, their visions, and their ministry, etc., and God was never in it.

God's not into *my* ministry, I've got to make sure I'm into His. His direction can be found in the still, small voice. Clear the clutter and listen for it.

THE LEADERSHIP OF GOD

*"But the Lord was not in the earthquake, and... the Lord was not in the fire; and after the fire, a still small voice." –*1 Kings 19:12

To clearly discern and recognize the leadership of God in our lives, we have to learn how to distinguish between what's in our emotions (what's in our soul) and what's in our intellect (reasoning).

Let's talk about how to recognize the *witnesses* of God, how to recognize the *leadership* of God, and conclude the *will* of God. Here's what happens: first, His Spirit bears witness with our spirit that we *are* the children of God. God wants to lead us more internally like this, yet at times there are external leaderships we shouldn't ignore. We'll talk about the distinction, but primarily, He leads us internally. Because of this, we can become confused when sorting between our emotions, our heads and God's voice.

Here's where a lot of people miss out: they're looking only for external leadership and completely miss the internal leadership. Why? Because they're looking for more of the *spectacular* leading of the Spirit through signs and external messages, and miss the more subtle, internal leading of the Spirit. Just because His internal leading is more subtle doesn't mean it's less supernatural.

Imagine me standing at a vending machine with 95 cents in my pocket and everything costs a dollar. I might be standing there thinking, "God, I really want this soda and I need a nickel. God, will You help me find a nickel?" Then all of a sudden, I felt impressed to move the garbage can, so I move the garbage can, and find a nickel laying there. I got my dollar, and I get what I want! Is that supernatural? Some might sit there and say, "No, that's a coincidence." Okay, then their philosophy or theology says it is a coincidence, but my philosophy and theology say it's Divine intervention into the natural, because the supernatural is when God steps out of the spirit realm into the natural realm, affecting our world. That is supernatural.

At what point does it become supernatural for you? Is it at 5 dollars? At 50 dollars? Is it 5 million? At what point? The more you learn to recognize the supernatural, and the more you normalize it, the more you grow in confidence and in recognizing God's leadership. But that's why many of us need *big* voices, *big* external leadership, we need spectacular signs, because we haven't learned how to develop the ear to hear His subtle leadership. Who doesn't want an angel to show up and tell them what to do? Bam! You're watching TV one afternoon, wasting time, and an angel appears in front of you unexpectedly, and you're trying to look around him, thinking, "Hey, I'm watching a football game right now!"

See, the reason we want the spectacular leading is because it allows us to be lazy in seeking God. We'd rather have a booming voice come from heaven, "THUS SAYETH THE LORD," as the house shakes. Then we'll say, "WOW, what do You want, God?" Again, we wish for these types of experiences because they require little of us.

DOORS

"For a great and effective door has opened to me, and there are many adversaries."
–1 Corinthians 16:9

We like the gifts of the Spirit; words of knowledge, or words of wisdom and prophesy. We like those external leaderships. We love to pray for open doors and for doors to close if it's not His will, and putting out fleeces, etc. You understand—we don't have to do a lot of work when that stuff happens.

Paul said, one time, for those of you who want to have open or closed doors, you think an open door is like the yellow brick road. Paul said on one occasion, "For a great and effective door has opened to me, and there are many adversaries." Well, if I open a door and I feel the adversaries coming, then I'm going to close it. You know what I'm talking about! I'll say, "Wow, there's monsters out there, I'm going to close the door. There's a storm out there...let's close the door."

Whenever God opens doors for me, it's usually a lot of work, it's a lot of stress, a lot of problem-solving, a lot of growing up. Please close the door! But I've had to learn to walk through the doors that God has opened for me, and to recognize these more subtle leadings of the Spirit. When we do this, we grow in confidence in Him.

We take the Word, we take the external leadership, we take the internal leadership, and they become witnesses to us. God says, "In a multitude of counselors there is safety." We take these witnesses and conclude His will in our lives. We're going to go through them systematically. They don't break down in real life, but sometimes we have to break them down, pull them apart, understand, and recognize them.

When you are born again, you're going to learn and start recognizing the inner witness of God's Spirit in your life. In 1 John 2 verse 20 it says, "But you have an anointing," which means a divine enablement from the Holy One, "and you know all things." What God is saying, and the best example I can use, is when you pull out your computer that has Internet access, you can Google anything. Need information about something? Just Google it! God is saying, "When you get born again, you get My anointing, My Internet access, you can Google Me, and know anything you need to know. You want to know My will? You want to know My plan? You want to know My direction? Just Google Me. You have access."

RECOGNIZING DECEPTION

"These things I have written to you concerning those who try to deceive you." –1 John 2:26

How many know that not everyone is a peer? Not everyone is who they appear to be. Many of us have relationships we should not continue to cultivate. Why? Because some relationships are not good for our destiny.

There are also business deals we should not get into because God is trying to lead us and guide us away from those deals. He knows they'll end badly. On the other hand, sometimes there are things, opportunities or circumstances that don't make sense to our natural minds, yet God is saying, "You need to pursue this." In both cases, we need to learn to recognize His voice, so that Satan doesn't deceive us.

Anointing—there's that word again; a divine enablement you receive from God that abides within you. Where is it? Within. How's God going to lead you? Internally. **The anointing of God abides in you, and His Spirit will teach you.**

TRUSTING GOD WITH FINANCES

*"Give, and it will be given to you: good measure,
pressed down, shaken together and running over."*
–Luke 6:38

At times, what we think and what we feel are opposite. Our intellect can say stop, and our emotions can say go. One of the places you'll experience this, oftentimes, is at offering time. You may not feel like giving and/or you may not think it's a good time to give.

I remember a time, as a young believer in my early twenties, when I had $5 dollars in my pocket, and I needed gas. In those days, $5 dollars was not a gallon of gas; it filled up the whole tank! Yes, it was *way* back. That $5 dollars meant I could get to and from work for the next week, and there were still several days to go before payday.

I felt that little nudge in my spirit saying, "*Give* that $5 dollars." Now, I know this was not my emotion, and I know this wasn't my head either, because both of them would certainly be saying NO! So I said, "Okay God, this is freaking me out, because you understand, God, if I run out of gas, I'm walking." It wasn't a life or death deal; I was in my twenties and I suppose I could have walked to work. It was just a little, normal life thing.

So I said, "Okay God, I'll give my $5 dollars." As soon as the offering bucket had passed by, a man sitting in the pew in front of me immediately turns around and says, "God told me to give this to you." I gave my $5 dollars. He did not give me $100 dollars; he did not give me $50 dollars; he did not give me $10 dollars; I did not get a hundred-fold return that day. He gave me $5 dollars. **However, at that moment, I knew I could trust God.**

Recently, God put it on my heart to build a barn on a piece of property the church owns out in the country. God wanted me to trust Him. If I hadn't learned to trust God during the small tests, like the story of the $5 dollars, then I would never know how to trust Him with the bigger things in my life.

Some of us miss the leadership of God that is subtle, and that's why we need the bigger external things to occur. Practice following the more subtle things of God's leadership in your life, and it builds confidence within you and gives new perspective. Because, then, in your theology, even when God gives you a nickel, it's His supernatural intervention. If you recognize His help with little things, you'll be confident He'll also help you with big things. But if you don't know a God that helps you with little things, then you won't believe in a God that will help you with large needs. Are you catching this?

DESTINATION OF MATURITY

"The testing of your faith produces patience…that you may be perfect and complete, lacking nothing."
–James 1:3-4

The will of God is not a destination. Really, understanding the will of God is about the journey of getting there. For example, did we build a barn at our Solid Rock Ranch property as a church, or did the barn build us as a church? How many know that the destination of building a barn was not God's objective for us? Instead, it was *how* the barn built *our faith*.

There were people who believed, there were people who served, there were people who prayed, there were people who trusted, there were people who labored, and there were people who stepped out in faith with giving. All of a sudden, that process of getting to the destination grew each of them. So, I want you to recognize that it is not the destination; it's the journey that is valuable.

By faith we're going to build a new sanctuary, because I really believe that's the direction and destination of God in our hearts. But the spiritual goal is not a sanctuary. **The true goal is to *grow a people who will build a sanctuary.*** See, God gives us destinations to aim at. He gives us Promise Lands to believe for. He gives us hopes and dreams, but all the while His goal for us is to grow and mature, and turn into the person He created us to be, through all that the journey will require of us.

Can you see it?

THE AUDIBLE CALL

"Then the Lord called yet again, 'Samuel!'"
–1 Samuel 3:6

I want to talk about the inner voice of the Spirit. It can be even more than a *check* or a *nudge;* at times it is a very authoritative voice. The Spirit can come with an audible voice. If you study scripture, what sometimes appears to be an audible voice may not actually be audible to everyone nearby, but to the person God is speaking to, it's very audible.

Remember the story in the book of 1 Samuel? Samuel was lying in bed one night and he hears this voice call his name, "Samuel, Samuel." He jumps up and runs to the other room and says to Eli, "Here I am, for you called me." Eli did *not* hear the voice. He said, "I didn't call you, go back to bed." Samuel goes back to bed and hears, "Samuel, Samuel," jumps up again, and runs back in to Eli. Someone is speaking to him, but it's a voice he doesn't recognize, yet.

Finally the third time, Eli caught on to what was happening and said to Samuel, "Go lie down; and it shall be, if He calls you [because I'm not hearing it], that you must say, 'Speak Lord, for your servant hears.'"

If you and I want to begin to distinguish and discern the will of God for our lives, we've got to start with prayers like this: "God, I'm ready to hear. God, I want to hear. God, speak, for Your servant hears."

I remember as a young believer, I was woken up one morning and an authoritative voice said, "Read the New Testament." I jumped up, wondering who was there! It startled me! And then I recognized that it was the voice of the Spirit. If someone else had been in the room, would they have heard it? No – it was an authoritative voice, audible to me. Likewise, in Eli's room, it wasn't what God wanted to say to Eli; it was what God wanted to say to Samuel. When you start recognizing the leading of the Spirit of God, you can sense when God is speaking to someone. But, you don't necessarily hear what God is saying to them.

In the life of the Apostle Paul, Acts chapter 9 tells the story of when he had an encounter with God. "And the men who journeyed with him stood speechless, hearing a voice, but seeing no one." So, in other words, his companions heard the voice, but when Paul re-counts that story in Acts 22, verse 6 says, "Now it happened, as I journeyed and came near Damascus at about noon, suddenly a great light from heaven shone around me. And I fell to the ground and heard a voice saying to me, 'Saul, Saul, why are you persecuting Me?' So I answered, 'Who are you, Lord?' And He said to me, 'I am Jesus of Nazareth, whom you are persecuting.' And those who were with me indeed saw the light and were afraid, but they did not hear the voice of Him who spoke to me."

It appears to be a contradiction, but it's not. God wasn't speaking to the others; it was a personal message to Paul about his new mission for life.

When the authoritative voice of the Spirit pierces right into you, it appears audible to you. When it pierces right into *you*, God's trying to set a course for *you*. It may even be preparing you for adversity to come. Sometimes adversity is ahead of you, and God knows you'll need an anchor to hang on to. Everyone goes through hard times; in ministry, in marriage, with kids, a crisis in our faith, etc., and we need hope and God's promises to keep us going. Those authoritative calls from God become the anchors you can hang on to.

AUTHORITATIVE VOICE

*"Jesus said, "Peace to you! As the Father has sent Me, I also send you." –*John 20:21

Have you ever asked God a question, because you felt something wasn't right in the world? At one of our recent men's conferences where we had several hundred men in attendance, one of our leaders, Brian Elliot, was in prayer. In his spirit, Brian was unsatisfied with the number of men who were not there.

"God, why aren't there 5,000 men in here?" Immediately, he felt like the Spirit of God shot right back to him and said, **"What are you going to do about it?"** Brian knew at that point that God was speaking to his heart, and since then, he's been on a journey. When he spoke at our next men's meeting, you could hear a new authority in his voice, and the men in the house are responding to the authority. An authoritative voice spoke into his spirit, and now Brian speaks with a new authority.

All of a sudden, when Brian talks now, men sit up, they straighten up, they perk up, and they pay attention, because there's an authority in his voice; because of the authority that was spoken into his spirit. As long as he follows that leading, the next season of his life will be filled with impacting the lives of thousands of men.

He has a call from the Spirit. Impacting the lives of 5,000 men will take him a while.

The reason a lot of people need to hear God often is because they don't like the last word they got. When God speaks to me, I know it's going to mean challenging work is ahead. There's no need for me to continue seeking more words from the Lord if I haven't done anything with the previous one.

WHO ARE YOU TALKING TO?

"Speak Lord, for your servant hears." –Samuel 3:9

God is drawing Samuel. God's authoritative voice is speaking to him, God is calling him, but Samuel doesn't know how to recognize the promptings of God. He doesn't know how to recognize the leadership of God. He doesn't know how to recognize the voice of God, and so he runs to Eli. God's calling Samuel, but he's running to Eli.

Sometimes when God starts doing things on the inside of you, they're not clear to you. When it's not clear, you will either run to somebody or something, hoping that whatever or whoever you run to will help you make sense out of what God is trying to say. The problem is that the person you're running to may not know God's voice in their own life.

Samuel did not know the voice of the Lord yet. Thank God, Eli recognized that God was calling the boy. What if he hadn't? Thankfully, Eli directed Samuel well, telling him to go lie down, and the next time he heard his name called, to say, "Speak Lord, for Your servant heareth."

Sure enough, God called Samuel again. Samuel said, *alright God you got my attention, and now where do you want to direct my attention?* That's wisdom right there. Are you catching it? Eli is giving good directions to the young boy, Samuel. Samuel is learning how to recognize that God is calling, learning to recognize how God is speaking, and learning *who* God is talking to.

Years ago, God starting speaking this kind of thought to me; about how to recognize people whom He is calling. I was learning to recognize people who God wanted to raise up and use. Here's the exciting thing: Samuel grew up to become the prophet to Israel, and recognizing God's voice went from being rare to being common for Samuel. He had the privilege of anointing the first two kings to come to that nation. So, as a boy, God had a marvelous plan for Samuel's life, but God first had to get Samuel's attention to direct him in all that He had for him.

RECOGNIZING LEADERS

"They were imploring us with much urgency that we would receive the gift of fellowship of the ministering to the saints." –2 Corinthians 8:4

One time while visiting another church, I said to the congregation, "I'm going to buy my ticket and watch what happens here. This church is going someplace, and God is doing something here." I sensed there was an important work of God going on in that church.

When we go into a church, we can sense if it's stagnant, right? It's like walking by a stagnant pond: no matter how thirsty we are, we won't drink from it. Also, if our personal faith is stagnant, people recognize it. If our walk with God is stagnant, people sense it. However, they also recognize when it's fresh.

I sensed there was something fresh and vibrant in that church. I continued, saying, "I know I'm a visitor today, but when I come back in the future, and I stand on the platform in your *new* building, in your *new* sanctuary, and all the new people look at me, thinking, "Who are you?" I'm going to say, "I was here before you were. I saw you before you got here.

I was here in your previous building, I was praying for you by faith, and I saw you, in this increased place, by faith." How would I have sensed that? I perceived that God's hand was on the leaders of that house, and the leaders of that house were moving forward and stepping out onto faith.

At CCC we have a ministry school called Formation. We schedule it during the middle of the day, and we charge money for people to enroll. People always wonder why we do it during the day, and why we charge money for it. There are strategic reasons.

I have found that there are many people who are *interested* in seeking God, but are not *committed* to seeking God. I want to know who is *hungry*. Who is too busy, but figures out how to adjust their schedules to come? Who doesn't have the money, but figures it out anyway? Because, if you've got no money now, and you can figure out how to pay for the classes, maybe you'll have a multi-million dollar building project in the future and you'll figure it out successfully. If you don't have the time now, but end up fitting it in somehow, maybe you can make it work when you're managing multiple church locations and multiple services someday. But if you can't figure it out with your current problems, you won't be able to solve the higher-level problems in the future.

Now, I understand it's not for everybody, but I'm trying to recognize and perceive who God is calling, and then help them learn to recognize and distinguish His leadership in their life.

POSITIONED TO LISTEN

"I still have many things to say to you, but you cannot hear them now." –John 16:12

For God to start speaking to you, put yourself into a position where you can start hearing from God. Remember when Moses turned aside to see the burning bush and heard a voice? God was speaking to him. In other words, God is not going to speak to us until He has our attention. After God got Moses' attention, Moses went into a dialog with God.

Remember the story about Elijah, when God was not in the wind, and God was not in the earthquake, and God was not in the fire, but God was in a still small voice? And when Elijah heard that still small voice, he went out and wrapped his face in his *mantle*. His *mantle* was a robe that he carried, but it was symbolic of his ministry. He went to the edge of the cave, put on his mantle, and all of a sudden God's still small voice begins speaking to him, and a dialog starts to occur. Until God starts capturing your attention, He has things He wants to say to you that He's *not* saying.

In John 16, Jesus goes on to say, "However, when He, the Spirit of Truth, has come, He will guide you" [not tell you, but guide you], "into all truth; for He will not speak in His own authority, but whatever He hears He will speak; and He will tell you things to come." The Spirit will guide you into truth, but He won't necessarily tell you exactly where you're going. Some of us want God to tell us all the details, but he says, "No, I'll guide you." It's a life of discovery; it's a life of maturity; it's a life of growing; it's a life of trust.

Jesus also promises in John 14, "But the Helper, the Holy Spirit, whom the Father will send in my name, He will teach you all things and bring to your remembrance all things that I said to you." What will He do? The Spirit will teach you and remind you of truth.

It's in the positioning of yourself to listen that dialogs with God occur, then God can speak life-altering revelation to you.

HE IS BUILDING

"Unless the Lord builds the house, they labor in vain who build it." –Psalm 127:1

This series of events is one of the most profound and defining moments of my life. In 2003, before we bought the property where our church is now, I was driving through the nearby intersection having a time of prayer with God. If I'm honest, it wasn't really a time of prayer, it was more a time of complaining. We were bursting at the seams at the location we had at the time, and I had been calling real estate agents to try to find a new building. We needed to grow, expand the ministry, grow the church, and build *the church*. I couldn't even get people to return my phone calls. Trying to make something happen was frustrating.

I remember saying out loud, "God, I'm just trying to build your church." I felt this authoritative voice come right back saying, "I did not ask you to build My church." I've never had a thought like that in my life. I had spent years building the church I was pastoring. My whole life had been about building. My first thought was *the devil is in my car*!

It was like I was having a moment from the movie *The Matrix*. Life just slowed down, because before I passed through the intersection right here where the building is now, with no thought about owning this building, He responded to me, "I did not ask you to build My church." Then I heard, "*I* will build My church." And then, I knew He was speaking to me.

In my frustration, I was mad and said, "Well, what do You want me to do?" God can handle our weary responses, and He can still reveal things. Trust me, He wants you to know His will, and He'll help you to pause and listen. He answered with revelation from Matthew 20, "I just want you to go and make disciples."

I cannot tell you the weight that came off of me that day. You just want me to help people, God? You want me to encourage people? You want me to teach people? Oh yes, I can do that! Then the peace and the presence of God filled my car. I said, "I'm going to stop striving to build this thing. I'm going to go and just start growing people. Okay God, if I can't find a building, I'm going to go and find pastors, and if I can't grow my church by a thousand people, I'll help build the Kingdom of God by helping *them* grow their churches." Soon after, I started a mentoring group called Pastors Network.

He had the burden of building, and I couldn't have foreseen what He was orchestrating next.

HE IS
ORCHESTRATING

*"For it is God who works in you both to will and to
do for His good pleasure."* –Philippians 2:13

My pursuit had become solely focused on developing
people. Not that I wasn't developing people before,
but a new clarity and focus sparked a new vision.
That same week, I walked into our previous location,
and a man who appeared to be homeless was
approaching me. My mind figured he wanted bus
money, but he says, "Are you the pastor?" "Yes," I
replied. "I own an apartment building down the alley
near the church, and I was going to sell it, but I
thought I would just come ask if the church would
want to buy it."

I hadn't been praying for an apartment building, it
had never crossed my mind, but the minute he said it,
something inside me prompted me, pushed me, to
learn more. To make a long story short, we bought it
with no money down, it had cash flow, and we picked
up 60,000 dollars of equity. I didn't want to be a
property manager, and it was in pretty rough shape.

At a Wednesday night service a few months later, I

said, "Church, I feel that God gave us this apartment complex and I don't know what to do with it. I just feel there's a higher purpose for it." The very next day, a local "at risk kids" agency contacted us who needed apartments for kids in their program. As kids moved in, the agency said, "This place is in pretty bad shape. Would it be okay if we helped you get a $100,000 dollar grant to help remodel it?" We got a grant, remodeled it all, and a few years later, the agency bought it from us. Praise the Lord! The Lord put the property in our hands...to grow people!

A few months later, we received a letter about a property for sale: it was the 60 acres adjacent to our kids camp, and would we want to bid on it. The gentleman who owned it was going into a nursing home, and his children were selling the property. We did not have the money at the time, but there was that inner prompt again. *Do this thing. Go forward.* We bid, and we bought the property. He looked over all the bids that came in and chose us. There was no way for us to get into a bidding war with the many developers and corporations who wanted it, but he decided to take our humble offer of $240,000.

Before we made *any* improvements, it appraised at $960,000. A year later, we got our new church building. All of these things happened within a few short years. Our property development and expansion exploded. We went from not being able to get a return call to having an explosion of property opportunities, all because we chose to follow God's leading to develop people and let Him build His church.

KINGDOM RESOURCES

"Most assuredly, I say unto you unless someone is born of water and of the Spirit, he cannot enter the Kingdom of Heaven." –John 3:5

I used to love football, I mean *love* football. I didn't like watching football with anybody else in the room, because they'd try to talk to me, distracting my focus. Then something changed: I got born again. God started calling me, and I started having new desires rising up within me; desires that conflicted with football. I was miserable. Do you have any clue what I'm talking about?

Nicodemus said to Jesus, "How can a man be born again when he is old? Can he enter the second time into his mother's womb?" In other words, he doesn't understand…how does this born again thing work? Jesus said, "Most assuredly, I say unto you unless someone is born of water and of the Spirit, he cannot enter the Kingdom of Heaven." Notice He said *enter* the Kingdom.

Now let me ask you a couple of questions. Do you live in a house or in an apartment? Do you own a car?

This morning you went to your closet and pulled out clothes that you put on today. Understand that all of those things and others like them were made from the resources of *this* kingdom; of this natural world. The resources of this natural kingdom created what's real in your world.

Your house is real from the resources of this kingdom. Your car is real from the resources of this kingdom. Your clothes are real from the resources of this kingdom. But before they became real, they were seen in someone's mind. I envisioned that house, so I created a plan, and I built it with natural resources available to me. Someone imagined that car, created a plan, and used the resources to build it. A seamstress or designer first saw the clothes design and then used tangible resources to create it. So the visible comes from the invisible, using the resources that are available to bring it to life.

First you have to enter the kingdom of this world (be born into it). Next, your reality in this world is created from this kingdom's resources.

When you and I get born again, we enter the Kingdom of God. When this happens, God says there are supernatural resources available to us. If we will use those resources, we'll start recognizing them more and more, allowing us to create from the invisible what becomes visible, or what becomes real in our lives.

I am a completely different person than I was before I

got born again. Along my journey, I began to use the available resources of the Kingdom to change, renew my mind and live a different kind of life, with different kinds of relationships, with a different approach to life, a different attitude about life, and a different philosophy about life. These new, God-centered perspectives have served me very well.

SHAPED BY THE SPIRIT

"That which is born of the flesh, is flesh. That which is born of the Spirit, is spirit. Do not marvel that I say you must be born again. The wind blows where it wishes and you hear the sound of it. You cannot tell where it comes from and where it goes. So is everyone who is born of the Spirit." –John 3:6-8

Have you ever visited the beach and seen the curious trees growing there? Trees on the sea cliffs that are continuously living in the strong ocean winds?

When I look at them, I've noticed none of their branches reach toward the ocean: all branches are pointed inland. I've been at the beach and looked at trees that look like they're in an incredible hurricane or typhoon, even when there's no wind at that moment. That kind of shaping of the tree does not occur in *one* windstorm. That kind of drastic shaping of the tree occurs from a life of living in the wind.

God's Spirit is like this ocean wind. You may not see the wind, but you can hear it rushing by. How does faith come? The Bible says faith comes by hearing. You don't see the wind, but you hear it and see the influence of the wind. You can see how it shapes everything living in its path.

When you and I are born again, here's what happens. All of a sudden we begin to hear the sound of His Spirit. As we begin to turn to it, we're repositioned and our perspective begins to change. What we start looking at starts changing us. This journey, our walk of faith, begins.

We start leaning into this thing called the Spirit. We walk by faith now and not by sight. Our perspective is different. Hope starts rising up in us, and confidence, too. We start thinking things are going to turn around. The more we enter into it, our desires begin to pursue it, and it begins to shape us. **Our life gets shaped by living in the Spirit's wind.**

I never thought I would be a pastor. I never thought I would live the life I am living. But I got born again and I turned into the wind of His Spirit, and He's been shaping me ever since. It's been the best choice I've ever made.

Choose to establish yourself in it. The wind is blowing, but many choose to avoid the wind. The wind is blowing, and a lot of people take shelter *from* the wind. But when you're born again, you look for that wind. See it and enter it.

FINDING PURPOSE

"The preparations of the heart belong to man, but the answer of the tongue is from the Lord."
–Proverbs 16:1

Our spirit speaks to us through the desires of our heart. The voice of your spirit sounds like the deepest desires of your heart. I am not talking about the desires of the flesh or our own foolish desires. I am talking about your purpose.

The Bible says in Proverbs 16, "The preparation of the heart belongs to us." It's my responsibility to prepare my heart. That's *my* part. My part is to prepare my heart. I hear the wind; I turn to the wind. I've turned to the wind; now I'm looking to respond to the wind. It's my job to prepare my heart. But now, here's God's part: "But the answer of the tongue is from the Lord." **I have a part – God has a part.**

"All the ways of man are pure in his own eyes." As I prepare, I should also examine my motives, but the Lord weighs the spirit. God's part is to give me feedback on my motives. Proverbs says, "A man's heart plans his way, but the Lord directs his steps."

Please catch this. It is so important that you understand this. So many sincere believers are just waiting for God to tell them what to do, and God says, "Where's your preparation? Where's your plan? *Why* do you want this?" You say, "I'm just waiting for you to answer me, God. God says, "Well, I answer a plan. I answer preparation. I answer the motives of your heart. Show Me your plan, and I will speak to you."

How many know that relationships consist of two people. You are in a relationship with God, and God says, "I want you to prepare your heart. I want you to look at the motives in your heart. And I want to see your plan." That is *our* part. Here's God's part, "I will answer you. I will examine your motives, give you feedback, shape your thoughts, and I will direct your steps."

Do you know how encouraging that is? It's encouraging to any person who will learn to lean into the Spirit and start walking by faith.

TAKE A RISK

"Then he who had received the one talent came and said, 'Lord, I knew you to be a hard man, reaping where you have not sown, and gathering where you have not scattered seed. And I was afraid, and went and hid your talent in the ground. Look, there you have what is yours.'" –Matthew 25:24-25

Many of us do not walk by faith because we are afraid. Because this is true, we need to realize that it's not faith, but fear, that shapes our life. We remain stagnant, hiding behind, "Well, God, I'm waiting on You, and just seeking You. I don't want to disappoint You. I don't want to fail You, and God, I don't want to let You down." This kind of thought process is rooted in fear.

Your spirit is crying out, "Turn to the wind! Turn and enter the Kingdom!" And you say, "But I don't see it...if I can't see it, I won't invest myself."

Think of it like this: instead of "God, I don't want to let You down, fail You, disappoint You or make a mistake...," consider the servant who received one talent from his master and then promptly hid his talent because he didn't want to risk losing it. He did not want to risk disappointing anyone, and he didn't want to risk failure.

A no-risk strategy is the riskiest strategy of all. Please internalize and hear what I just said. It was the poorest strategy possible for the one-talent servant because he lost, he disappointed, and he failed. Often, what we think is a no-risk or low-risk strategy is really the riskiest strategy of all. You've heard the saying, "No risk, no reward." In this case, it's certainly true plus even more dire results. His no-risk strategy and inaction brought punishment.

Seeing comes from the unseen. I'd rather disappoint God by trying my absolute best to walk by faith and missing the mark, than to say, "God, I did nothing because I didn't want to disappoint You," only to realize it was fear and not faith that was actually guiding my life.

HONOR GOD IN THE PROCESS

"For we walk by faith, not by sight."
–1 Corinthians 5:7

In my life, I've decided to turn to the wind and step into the wind of God's Spirit. I have allowed it to shape me for many years, and I understand how to start walking by this thing called *faith*. As a person seeks God for purpose, what if they take on a God-honoring process and do things like this:

They'll sit down and say, "God, here's what I sense Your Spirit saying. I just sense the promptings of Your Spirit.

"God, here are the desires of my heart. Here's what's in my heart, God. And here's what Your Word says about that.

"And, when I've asked wise men or women that I respect, here's their counsel on that.

"Here are the manifestations (if there have been any) I've seen, and God, here are my circumstances, and the opportunities that have been presented to me.

"So I am taking all these things, God, and I've prepared my heart and I've made a plan. Here is my plan.

"I am going to engage this plan, but here's what I am asking You: to answer me, examine me, and change me if you don't like it. Otherwise, I'm turning into the wind, and I'm going to assume this is Your will, and I am going forward."

DELIGHT YOURSELF IN THE LORD

"Delight yourself in the Lord, and He shall give you the desires of your heart." –Psalm 37:4

The Bible says in Psalm 37:4 "Delight yourself in the Lord, and He shall give you the desires of your heart." Now, I've been around church a long time, and a lot of people know just enough of the Bible to really mess themselves up!

When they get in trouble, they're about to go to jail, their spouse is about to leave them, or they've got something really bad about to happen to them, they know this verse in the Bible and think, "If I delight myself in the Lord, He's going to get me out of trouble." So they come to God with a desire to be rescued, saved and helped and there is nothing in and of itself that's wrong with that.

It often leads to a desperate effort: I'm going to pray and start going to church every time the doors are open and be *all in*, trying to earn His help and love. Many of us try to earn this, by, for a season, completely dedicating our life and time to God. So then, the case gets thrown out of court, the spouse

93

decides to come home, the body gets healed, and the problem is solved, they say, "Okay God, I'll see You next time I need You. I don't need to delight in You now because I got my desire."

But, if the problem isn't solved to their satisfaction, another attitude arises. "I served and I prayed and I read and I quoted, I am doing all the right things, then they say, "God, you let me down!" And the truth is they *never* delighted in God. **They had a *desire* that they delighted in and tried to use God to get it.**

That doesn't work, because God knows the motives of our hearts. And He's not for sale, nor can He be manipulated. It might work on people, but God says, "I know your heart. Don't use Me. I'll help you. If your life sucks, I'll help. If it's broken, I'll help. You need rescuing? I'll help. You're hurting? I'll help. But don't do the *use Me* thing, because I know the motives of your heart."

I have discovered an important truth to help me delight myself in the Lord. Rather than pursuing and delighting myself in blessings, things or accomplishments, my goal is to pursue a Person: the Lord. He shall supply all my needs. I recalibrate my heart to delight myself in Him only, and put even His blessings and benefits as secondary to loving Him.

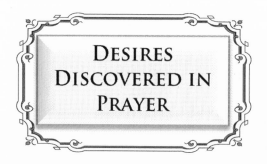

DESIRES DISCOVERED IN PRAYER

"May He grant you according to your heart's desire and fulfill all of your purpose." –Psalm 20:4

When you delight yourself in God, what kind of desires start rising up out of your heart? Mark 11:24 in the King James Version says, "Whatsoever things you desire when you pray..." When you *start* praying...when you're a believer, when you're born again, you're going to want to pray.

When you start praying, what kind of desires start coming up in your heart? When you start delighting in God, and praying, "God I enjoy you and I'm meditating on You, and I'm thinking about You, and I'm grateful for You..." When you start praying like that, what kind of desires start trying to perk up in your heart? When you start worshiping, singing worship unto God, singing in His presence, what kind of desires start trying to rise up on the inside of you?

See, those are the desires being born out of delighting in God. Not the desires that we try to use God for, but the desires that are emerging from delighting in God. What *are* those desires? Take note of them – they're

95

your spirit trying to lead you to align with God. That's your spirit trying to speak to you.

There are desires that are only going to arise out of being in His presence. How do I know this? I never wanted to go to church until I started getting in His presence. When I first started going to church it was because I felt broken. But then, I experienced His love and healing and that started drawing me deeper into Him. I didn't come to Him because my life was all together; I came to Him because my life needed to be redeemed. Then I began enjoying His presence and I started enjoying His Word and enjoying His people. That drew me deeper into Him, and He started pulling out of me what was in me. And there are desires within you that you'll never ever know until you start delighting in Him.

Psalm 20:4 says it this way, "May He grant you according to your heart's desire and fulfill all of your purpose." It came to me one day, how can God fulfill my heart's desire and my purpose at the same time unless they are same thing? Please catch that! Some people think to themselves, "If I go for the purposes of God, I have to give up my desire, and I lose my purpose. But if I go for my desires I have to give up my purpose, and I lose my purpose." No, not so. It's not one or the other.

When you hear the wind of His Spirit and your heart begins to respond to the wind of His Spirit and it begins to shape you, then you find that is your heart's desire, and you find that it's your purpose. When you start listening to the Spirit, you start listening to your heart's desire. And when you start listening to your heart's desire, you start discovering your purpose.

Someone should be excited about that thought, because if you understood it, why wouldn't you want to seek God eagerly, right now?

DEEP CALLS TO DEEP

"The purposes of a person's heart are deep waters."
–Proverbs 20:5

I never thought I'd be a pastor, I never thought I would do what I do with my life. God never forced or talked me into any of my work. I just continued turning into His Spirit, and He kept shaping me. Looking back, He wasn't asking me to do something that wasn't already in my heart. He was actually *pulling out of my heart* what I was created to do; allowing me to recognize it.

Had I not turned to Him, had I not entered His Kingdom, I would have never found this calling. Is this making any sense? **You should never die with potential in you**. Die with failure, but don't die with potential. If you're not born again, you'll never tap into what your full potential could be.

When you start sensing God's call, you start delighting in His presence; something is going to start to happen on the inside of you. Listen to what it says in Psalm 42:7, "Deep calls to deep." Do you know there are mysteries to be discovered in God? Yes, and there are also secrets in God. The Bible says, "Eye has not seen nor ear heard, neither has it entered into the heart of man the things which God has prepared for those who love Him, but He has revealed them to us by His Spirit." This scripture is saying that something deep inside of *us*, when it is born again, starts responding to that mystery, to that deep thing in *God*.

And that deep thing in God our Creator starts calling to the deep thing in us; the deep thing we were created for. The Bible says in Proverbs 20:5, "The purposes of a person's heart are deep waters." Did you hear that? He's trying to call you for what you were created for and call your purposes into existence.

It's like a tuning fork...the Spirit of God says something, your heart says something...the Spirit of God says something, your heart says something. When those two things start dialing in:

It's dialing in your heart's desire.
It's dialing in your deepest purpose.
It's dialing in what you were created for.

You don't even know it, you can't even see it but your Creator is trying to pull out of you what you were created for. Deep calls unto deep.

"Deep calls unto deep at the noise of Your waterfalls;
All Your waves and billows have gone over me."
–Psalm 42:7

Psalm 42:7 describes experiencing God. It says that the roar of "Your waterfalls," Your presence, and all Your waves and breakers have swept over me. How many know that when you turn into the wind of His Spirit something supernatural begins to sweep over you?

I want you to know that part of our relationship with God is not just intellectual, it's experiential! You begin to experience His presence, you begin to experience His goodness in your life, and you come into His presence, and He begins to wash over you.

There are defining moments in His presence. Remember Elijah the prophet? When Elijah was alone on the mountain, God was not in the strong wind that shook the rocks. God was also not in the earthquake, nor was God in the fire, but all of a sudden there was a still small voice. What did Elijah do? He knew that was God speaking and went down and covered himself up because it shook him to his core. When he heard that voice of the Spirit of God, it washed over him: it just flooded over him. Are you catching this?

There are times in God's presence when all of a sudden you may feel a new authority start rising up in you. You'll start praying with some kind of boldness, or you'll be in His presence and you'll just begin to weep as you meditate on His goodness. Or you'll be in His presence and it just rolls over you and an unexplainable confidence starts rising up in you. You start believing and saying, "It's going to be alright, it's going to be alright."

You'll feel these things start rising up in you because His presence is rolling over you, and He's washing through you. His deep is calling out to your deep.

GOD LOVES US WHERE WE ARE

"So I said: 'Woe is me, for I am undone! Because I am a man of unclean lips...'" –Isaiah 6:5

I want to tell you a story from the book of Isaiah, Chapter 6. The prophet Isaiah was in the presence of God. It says, "In the year that King Uzziah died, I saw the Lord sitting on His throne high and lifted up, and the train of His robe filled the temple. Above it stood seraphim; each one had six wings: with two he covered his face, with two he covered his feet, and with two he flew. And one cried to another and said: 'Holy, holy, holy is the Lord of hosts; the whole earth is full of His glory!'" In other words, His wind is blowing, His wind is blowing... "And the posts of the door were shaken by the voice of him who cried out."

How many of you know God's presence shakes things to their core? The seraphim cried out and the house was filled with smoke; the smoke of God's presence. "So I said: 'Woe is me, for I am undone!'"

When you start getting in God's presence it's easy to wonder, "Am I in the wrong place right now?" You begin to realize that:

He is great…and I am not so great.
He's amazing…I am less than amazing.
He is good…I am not good.
He is righteous…I am not righteous.

Do you know what I am talking about? You come into His presence and you say, "Oh my God, what am I doing here?! I do not belong here!"

God loves us where we are. Even so, we have to admit we are sinners before we can be born again. **For us to establish the right kind of relationship with Christ in our life, we must acknowledge our need for Him.** Then He can establish His rightful authority in our life.

Jesus died for everybody. But, only those who will admit they need Him will experience His grace and mercy.

But the passage doesn't end there. Isaiah says, "I am a man of unclean lips, and I dwell amongst a people of unclean lips." He's talking about his mouth, realizing he doesn't have a very good mouth. "For my eyes have seen the King, the Lord of hosts. Then one of the seraphim flew to me, having in his hand a live coal which he had taken with the tongs from the altar. And he touched my mouth with it and said: 'Behold, this has touched your lips; your iniquity is taken away, and your sin is purged.'"

In His presence, we see all our stains and we may feel like escaping His presence, but God starts removing all shame, all the guilt, and all of the embarrassment and sense of failure. Then you realize I don't belong here, but He loves me anyway. I'm not so great, but He is and He notices me. And while He's the King, He acknowledges my presence and chooses me.

Isaiah goes on to say, "And then I heard the voice of the Lord saying, 'Whom shall I send, and who will go for Us?'" So, from the presence of God, here comes the wind of His Spirit, "Whom shall I send, and who will go for Us?"

"Then I said," (says the guy who could not speak, but God touched his lips and buried his greatest iniquity) "Here am I! Send me."

HEART CONDITION

*"Keep your heart with all diligence, for out of it spring the issues of life." –*Proverbs 4:23

Here's the truth: when you're digging for your heart's desires, not everything that begins to come out of your heart is good. **When God starts calling, not everything that comes out of your heart is good.** That's why the Bible says in Proverbs 4:23, "Keep your heart with all diligence."

In other words, I've got a responsibility for everything that's in my heart. It is my garden. My heart is my property. For out of it spring the issues of life. And when God starts calling you, often before the voice of your spirit gets developed, there's a bunch of junk that starts coming up first.

Think about trying to get something pumped out of a well. Usually the first water that emerges isn't the *best* water. You're trying to get this thing pumped, you're trying to get this thing moving, and you've got to get this thing cleaned out. But the smelly, stagnant junky water is all you're getting at first. But we need to be discerning. In other words, prepare your heart,

107

do the best you can with checking your motives, then submit it to the Lord.

I have a grandson, little Ethan. He doesn't have words yet, and you can watch him getting so frustrated. Things will be happening and he'll be trying to tell you something, but he doesn't have words. So he'll be yelling, "Uh, uh, ah!" You can just see the frustration in his face as he is trying to express himself.

We, too, struggle: we're struggling because it's the junk that starts coming first out of our hearts. Our fears start coming, our failures start coming, our shame starts coming, our insecurities start coming. But God says, "Just keep it coming, we *will* get to the good stuff."

"Oh, but that's all bad stuff so far!" Just get it out because God's got to have the *whole* heart. And as long as you don't get it out, it just stays on top of the treasure.

See, that's also why God gives us the incredible gift of praying in the Spirit. Do a study on that, because when you pray in the Spirit, you speak the mysteries of God. When you pray in the Spirit, you pray those things and the Holy Spirit is saying, "I understand your spirit doesn't have words yet. Let me give you some words so you can pray through the *junk*."

The other day, I was with Ethan. We were getting ready to leave and we're saying, "Bye." And he got it,

"Bye." So, for the next ten minutes, we're saying, "Bye, bye, bye!" and we're waving, and he's happy. He's got a word! He's got a word! Not frustration, but joy came to him this time, because he got a word!

Some of you are looking for a word from God. Maybe you need a word from your own spirit that hasn't been able to speak your whole life yet. Prime the pump, and get the junk out!

JUNK YARD WALK

"So he said to Him, 'Oh my Lord, how can I save Israel? Indeed my clan is the weakest in Manasseh, and I am the least in my father's house."
—Judges 6:15

Do you know the story of Gideon? Judges 6:12 says, "The angel of the Lord appeared to him and said, 'The Lord is with you, you mighty man of valor.'" Gideon turns to the presence of God, and what a word he gets from God!

"The Lord is with you, you mighty man of valor." The Lord didn't say, "Now watch your junk and your attitude that comes out while you're talking to Me..." Good thing, because Gideon replies, "Oh my Lord, if the Lord is with us, why did all this happen to us?" I love this. He is questioning the Creator. He's questioning God. Like God should explain to him how things are supposed to roll!

Gideon's frustration is talking. "If the Lord is with us, why has all this happened to us, and where, oh where, are Your big-deal miracles? Did not the Lord bring us up from Egypt? But now the Lord has forsaken us."

111

He's really saying, "It's *Your* fault." Now he's blaming God.

"You delivered us into the hands of our enemies, the Midianites." Now here comes the goodness of God: the Lord turned to him and said, "Go in the might of yours and use it to save Israel from the hands of the Midianites." He just came through all this junk, and the goodness of God was saying, "Come on, keep bringing it Gideon. Let it all out. Go in this might of yours." Gideon says, "I cannot save Israel. Indeed, my clan, my family is the weakest in Manessah."

God, have you seen my family? I've got the most dysfunctional family in all of Israel. And by the way, I'm the most dysfunctional person in the most dysfunctional family. I've got baggage. I got junk. I don't have what it takes. I don't think I can do this. And God says, "Okay, are you ready to let all of that stuff stop talking yet? Surely, I'll be with you."

Start your faith walk with all your junk. Start your faith walk with all your fears. That tree has been shaped by years and years of standing in the wind – it didn't happen overnight. It just chose to stay there and stay in the wind. Everything about it looks like a windstorm. Everything about your life can look like God has swept through your life, and He has shaped you for what He has called you for.

God knows there is junk in you, but He also knows the precious things hidden underneath.

TREASURE IN YOUR SPIRIT

"The Kingdom of Heaven is like a treasure hidden in a field, which a man found and hid, and for joy over it, goes and sells everything that he has and buys that field." –Matthew 13:44

I want you to think of Matthew 13:44 like this: you are the field. And in the field is a treasure. There's a treasure in you. There's a treasure in your spirit. There's a purpose in you; what you were created for. God says that what's in your field has such value that He's going to ransom heaven to purchase that field. God gave heaven's best to acquire you.

If you've ever seen the show on TV called "Storage Wars," it's about people who buy abandoned storage units. They get five minutes to look in the units (not actually stepping into them), they can't open anything, and they're looking for clues, guessing if there's anything valuable in there. Then they determine what they're going to bid on buying all the abandoned contents, and the highest bidder wins it. Then, the winner starts going through everything to find out if there's treasure there, something of value, and they start separating what they're going to throw away and what might be of value.

They learn to recognize what might be valuable, but they're not always sure. Maybe it looks old or antique, or the quality in which it was made is superb, or there's a well-known manufacturer's name that they recognize. If so, they'll take it to get an appraisal done.

God says, "I know the treasure in you and I'm willing to buy the whole unit. And let's just start sorting through the junk while looking for the treasure."

I saw an episode where a guy saw a safe in a unit, so he bought the unit. When he opened the safe, it was empty, and he was mad. One of the other guys comes by and says, "You're a moron. Do you understand what kind of safe that is? That safe is worth more than you paid for the whole unit." But he didn't know what he had. Some of us need to learn this same lesson and bring our hearts to God. We don't know the treasure we have already.

God, I'm not sure that this is worth anything, but here's my gift, here's my treasure, God. I'm not sure if this has any value, but would You appraise it for me, and would You put it back in circulation, because it's been buried, and it's been hidden, and I was afraid, and I was ashamed, and I was disappointed.

There is heavenly treasure in your spirit!

"HE WHO HAS AN EAR, LET HIM HEAR WHAT THE **SPIRIT SAYS** TO THE CHURCHES. TO HIM WHO OVERCOMES I WILL GIVE TO EAT FROM THE TREE OF LIFE, WHICH IS IN THE MIDST OF THE PARADISE OF GOD."

REVELATION 2:7

SMALL GROUP & BIBLE STUDY QUESTIONS

Would you enjoy studying and discussing GPS with your small group or Bible study group?

Use the following, easy to use, six-week group reading and discussion plan to encourage each other and share insights God has shown you while reading *GPS*:

Week One
Based on pages 13 – 27

Theme: *The Seven Ways God Speaks*

Questions:

1. When considering the seven ways God leads us, which one do I tend to look for/depend on the most? Why?

   He leads me most by his Spirit because when I feel it, I know its from him.

2. The result of obedience is joy. Why is this result important to have in my life?

   Because then I can reflect that onto others.

3. Describe a time when you have gotten into the ditch of being led by emotion or the other ditch of being stuck in your intellect. What was the outcome?

right now in my life I feel stuck because of my emotions keep me there.

4. Share an example of when you believe God's Spirit was speaking to you or leading you.

When I opened my barbershop ministry at the rescue mission in California.

Discussion Notes:

_____
_____
_____
_____
_____
_____
_____
_____
_____
_____
_____
_____
_____
_____
_____
_____
_____
_____
_____
_____

Week Two
Based on pages 29 – 43

Theme: *Moving Past Man's Wisdom*

Questions:

1. In my life now, how can I be a better steward of
   my time to "redeem" the time? Are there things
   God has asked of me that I haven't done yet?

   Become more clear minded of
   the things God asks of me, be obediant.

2. When I seek God, do I tend to seek Him for
   individual answers and needs, or to hear what He
   has to say to the body of Christ as a whole? Why?

   Right now In my life, I try to Seek
   individual answers to better myself because
   I feel I need direction.

3. In what way(s) does God use me for His
   purposes?

   To provide life skills and counsel
   for my children to help them through
   life.

4. Why is it important to seek Godly leadership and
   counsel in life? Who do I seek it from?

   Its important for me because Godly
   leadership is better than my own.
   It is important to listen to a mentor
   that is in tuned with Gods direction,
   for advice and direction. To get and
   o Share ideas and put things into
   motion.

118

Discussion Notes:

* Redeeming time "better listener"
asking God what he wants me
to do.

* Use knowledge learned through
fellowship to grow.

* Isaiah 6:8

Week Three
Based on pages 45 – 63

Theme: *Let God Lead*

Questions:

1. Have you ever felt God "check" or "nudge" your spirit, and you knew you were supposed to do something or not do something? Explain.

    Yes, when I started my ministry wasn't sure if it was God until I was Obedient and stepped out.

2. What is the clutter you need to cut through (mind, time, physical clutter, etc.) so that you're free to hear God's voice?

    depression and anxiety and time management.

3. Do you tend to think of knowing and doing God's will as a destination to arrive at, or a journey to travel? How does it affect your mindset?

    When you let God in, everything feels okay. Your Mindset Changes.

4. In what way(s) could you trust God with your finances more? Or, if you trust Him completely now, what did you used to struggle with in this area and how did you overcome it?

    trust God with the process of tithing

Discussion Notes:

_____

_____

_____

_____

_____

_____

_____

_____

_____

_____

_____

_____

_____

_____

_____

_____

_____

_____

_____

_____

_____

_____

_____

_____

_____

_____

_____

_____

_____

Week Four
Based on pages 65 – 79

Theme: *Position Yourself to Hear*

Questions:

1. Have you ever heard God's Spirit speak to you with an authoritative voice? What did He say?

   _No_ _____

   _____

2. Have you ever asked God a question, because you felt something wasn't right in the world? What was the question? Could God have work for you to do in this area?

   _____

   _____

3. Do you think it's difficult for God to get your attention? What could you do to make it easier?

   _____

   _____

4. What have you been striving for in life that seems to be a struggle, and God doesn't seem to be answering? Could God want you to be focusing on something else that's important to Him, and then He'll take care of what's missing for you?

   _____

   _____

Discussion Notes:

_____
_____
_____
_____
_____
_____
_____
_____
_____
_____
_____
_____
_____
_____
_____
_____
_____
_____
_____
_____
_____
_____
_____
_____
_____
_____
_____
_____
_____
_____

Week Five
Based on pages 81 – 95

Theme: *Shaped by the Spirit*

Questions:

1. God has supernatural resources available to us.
   Which of His resources do you need more of in
   your life to be effective for His purposes?

   _____

   _____

2. What conversation do you have with God when a
   decision needs to be made?

   Please God give me direction.

3. What does delighting yourself in the Lord mean to
   you?

   Being happy in his presence, feeling his presence throughout my mind.

4. Describe your life dream and one step you can
   take right now toward it.

   Starting a Ministry to help people feel good about they're accomplishments and Carreer establishment.

Discussion Notes:

_____

_____

_____

_____

_____

_____

_____

_____

_____

_____

_____

_____

_____

_____

_____

_____

_____

_____

_____

_____

_____

_____

_____

_____

_____

_____

_____

_____

_____

_____

Week Six
Based on pages 99 – 114

Theme: *Treasure in Your Spirit*

Questions:

1. Pastor Dave never thought he'd be a pastor. Has God shaped you in ways that you never would have expected? In what ways?

   He has transformed my heart and am now able to let go easier

2. Would you say your relationship with God so far has been more intellectual or experiential? Do you know him intellectually or do you experience Him?
   Why do you think that is?

   I know him itellectually, I seek him first and feel his presence daily.

3. Describe a gift/treasure you uncovered as you allowed God to get you past your "junk."

   I am a great leader of strength and wisdom.

4. How have you experienced God's forgiveness in your life?

   I have made several big mistakes and God has always answered prayers and leads a way no matter what I have done.

Discussion Notes:

Answer Questions to Others

40-Day Reading Plan

Enjoy *GPS* as a 40-day reading plan by following this recommended daily reading schedule:

Week one, read:
Introduction
Stay Out of the Ditch
Emotion and Intelligence
The Workmanship of God

Week two, read:
You Are Not Lost
Multitude of Counselors
An Ear to Hear
Times and Seasons
Be Useable
Redeem the Time
God's Expectations

Week three, read:
The Spirit Nudges
Cut Through the Clutter
The Leadership of God
Doors
Recognizing Deception
Trusting God with Finances
Destination of Maturity

Week four, read:
The Audible Call
Authoritative Voice
Who Are You Talking To?

Recognizing Leaders
Positioned to Listen
He is Building
He is Orchestrating

Week five, read:
Kingdom Resources
Shaped by the Spirit
Finding Purpose
Take a Risk
Honor God in the Process
Delight Yourself in the Lord
Desires Discovered in Prayer

Week six, read:
Deep Calls to Deep
Experience His Presence
God Loves Us Where We Are
Heart Condition
Junk Yard Walk
Treasure in Your Spirit

If you'd like to dive deeper into this topic, consider going through this book with others: start or join a small group, Bible study or book club, and use *GPS* as your study curriculum.

For additional copies of *GPS* for friends, family, Bible study groups, and military service members, please visit www.go2ccc.org or www.CreativeForcePress.com

Readers, if you've enjoyed this book, would you consider rating it and reviewing it on Amazon.com? Thank you.

About the Author

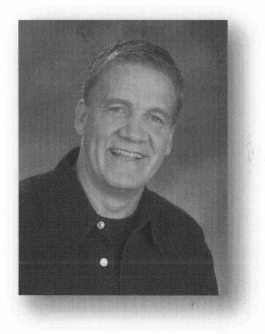

Pastor Dave Minton has been the senior pastor of Capital Christian Center (CCC) in Olympia, Washington, since 1989. Passionate about serving his community, local military personnel and ministry leaders, under the stewardship of Pastor Dave, CCC hosts free community events, military fellowship ministry, celebrate recovery, leadership seminars, ministries for children, youth, women and men, and offers more than eight services each week. Pastor Dave is married to Kelly, and together they have five grown children and two grandchildren.

GPS is proudly published by:

Creative Force Press
Guiding Aspiring Authors to Release Their Dream

www.CreativeForcePress.com

Do You Have a Book in You?

Made in the USA
Charleston, SC
02 February 2014